The Shogun Scrolls

Shogun no Rin

On Controlling All Aspects of the Realm

STEPHEN F. KAUFMAN, HANSHI 10TH DAN

CHARLES E. TUTTLE CO., INC.
Boston • Rutland, Vermont • Tokyo

First published in 1997 by Charles E. Tuttle Publishing, an imprint of Periplus Editions (HK) Ltd., with editorial offices at 153 Milk Street, Boston, Massachusetts 02109.

Library of Congress Cataloging-in-Publication Data

Kaufman, Steve, 1939–
    The shogun scrolls : on controlling all aspects of the realm / by Stephen F. Kaufman.
        p. cm.
   ISBN 0-8048-3122-X
   1. Education of princes—Japan. 2. Shoguns. 3. Minamoto, Yoritomo, 1147–1199. 4. Nakadai, Hidetomo. I. Title.
JC393.K38 1997
320.1—dc21   96-40265
                                                CIP

Distributed by

Charles E. Tuttle Co., Inc.
RR1 Box 231-5
North Clarendon, VT
05759-9700
Tel: (800) 526-2778
Fax: (800) FAX-TUTL

Tuttle Shokai Ltd.
1-21-13, Seki
Tama-ku, Kawasaki-shi 214
Japan
Tel: (044) 833-0225
Fax: (044) 822-0413

Berkeley Books Pte. Ltd.
5 Little Road #08-01
Singapore 536983
Tel: (65) 280-3320
Fax: (65) 280-6290

First edition
1 3 5 7 9 10 8 6 4 2   00 99 98 97

Design by Fran Kay
Printed in the United States of America

This is for my mother,
Dell Kaufman
You were right all along,
Absolutely!

CONTENTS

INTRODUCTION

*T*he ancient text from which this book is drawn is a hidden work that has recently come to light owing to my personal investigations into the teachings of Miyamoto Musashi's *Book of Five Rings* and Sun Tzu's *Art of War*. The *Shogun Scrolls* were written in the late twelfth century by Hidetomo Nakadai, a regent and scholar of no particular rank or importance other than being a samurai ("one who serves") in the court of the Minamoto clan and a retainer to Minamoto Yoritomo, the first shogun of Japan, who is considered to be one of world history's most ruthless and savage generals.

The entire country was in turmoil; countless coups, indescribable conspiracies and assassinations were everyday occurrences. It was during this period that the ninja became identifiable. Zen Buddhism had just been introduced into Japan from China by the priest Eisai, and it was already making its influence felt, creating religious strife as well. The Minamoto were fighting the Taira clan factions for control of the government, and warfare was constant. It was in this serious state of national debilitation that Nakadai, under constant query by Yoritomo for his thoughts and opinions regarding the state of affairs and rules of conduct in government, put his ideas in writing. Because of the precarious nature of his court position, Nakadai had to be sure that what he advised the first shogun of Japan was the utmost in correctness. He could make no mistakes if he valued his life.

During the course of history, there have been many attempts at similar "truths" revealed in different parts of the world. One is Machiavelli's *Prince,* written some three hundred years after the *Shogun Scrolls.* There is a major difference between *Shogun no Rin* and *The Prince.* Although he was unfairly banished in his own estimation, which might suggest an inability to maintain authority based on his own teachings, Machiavelli explains his understanding of the affairs of men and fate as the reason for writing his book. Nakadai, on the other hand, was held in very high esteem and did not have to qualify his philosophical position. He maintained himself in an ever higher position in his world and died a very rich and happy man, singularly honored by all who knew him and knew of his work.

Once past the introduction by Nakadai, which establishes proper etiquette and politeness, Yoritomo could study the rhyme and reason of men's actions in conducting their affairs and lives while comparing them to his own exploits based on the historical examples Nakadai used. Nakadai obviously had the experience and ability, as well as the respect of the court, to intelligently present these ideas to Yoritomo but begs forgiveness for his arrogance in telling the shogun how to conduct his affairs. He also suggests, with humility, that the words be read in the spirit in which they are written and the understanding that permits a man to realize his own greatness.

As a working philosopher and motivation lecturer, I am not interested in actual historical events that set the stage for the original writings. I am more concerned with the information and the understanding of it, which provides answers for every man. These scrolls should be used as a guide for personal progress through life, although it should be understood by the reader that certain ideas presented to the shogun in the twelfth century do not pertain to contemporary life and society, such as raping, looting, and revenge. I do not advocate raping and looting, and neither should anyone with an enlightened mind. I believe that the work is more important than the worker, until, of course, both become the same, and I have endeavored to structure my life based on the majority of the principles presented in the *Shogun Scrolls*.

As with many arcane works of profound philosophical value, the *Shogun Scrolls* has not had ample exposure. The reason, according to contemporary scholars, is that it would have given the reader of Nakadai's time a tremendous advantage in governing the realm. The severe penalties suggested by Nakadai for violators of the shogunate must have pleased Minamoto Yoritomo. He rewarded Nakadai with an entire fiefdom and elevated him to the position of *monchujo*, the equivalent of a seat on our own Supreme Court. Copies of the work that could be found were eventually destroyed with the exception of the four that exist today with the seal of Minamoto Yoritomo, indicating that they were the only copies to be kept. All others were to be destroyed. Anyone who had a copy was also to be destroyed—Nakadai's influence, undoubtedly.

Such is the profound importance of the work. The attitudes expressed in the *Shogun Scrolls* far exceed any of those works of literature that appear to emulate it. And so, here it is, presented to the world for the first time in nearly 800 years. Learn from it!

Stephen F. Kaufman, Hanshi
New York City 1996

A Gift to Minamoto Yoritomo
Shogun of All the Japans
from his most humble and loyal servant
Hidetomo Nakadai

My Liege,

You have suggested I advise you in matters of conducting the business of the realm. I beg your forgiveness for my intrusion into the affairs of great men such as yourself, but that you say I have proven myself to you over the long years through my service further gives me the honorable desire to serve you with all of my heart, mind, and soul for my entire life.

Please forgive my arrogance in thinking that I can put my ideas down for your consideration. I assure you that they are granted me by Heaven and that you are the only recipient of them.

May I suggest that the words be read with the true spirit of understanding that comes from my many years of contemplation on the ideas I am presenting. I humbly present my thoughts to you on the following matters and pray that you do not think of me as one who would consider himself as wise as you.

Your esteemed servant,
Hidetomo Nakadai

Chapter One

How Power Comes To Be

*P*ower comes to a man in various ways. Undoubtedly, it is granted to a man by his own personal choice. It is based on his desire to rule or to be ruled. The extent to which that desire is expressed will be made manifest in his life. It does not matter if it is the desire to control an entire country or a desire to control a small faction with a private interest. It depends on a man's thoughts and the manner in which he accepts the truth of his own greatness.

Such was the thinking of your brother, Yoshitsune, when he wrested control from the Taira clan. He observed their obvious weaknesses, which became more evident when they expressed a preference to live the aristocratic life and forgot the ways of the warrior. They forgot how they took control from the Fujiwara clan and soon became arrogant and slovenly in their attitudes and actions. Your brother imposed his desire on those circumstances, and it permitted him to become a great general.

Power is a private matter, recently structured as new or passed from generation to generation, being subject to the fates and a man's desire. The civil domain is maintained by means of subjecting the population by force, irrespective of appearance, and only works when there is respect for the leader. It does not matter if this respect is in the form of love or fear. Leaders maintain power by a consensus of opinion and the timely showing of strength: their own. As shogun, you control the entire country, and should anyone interfere with your authority they should be eliminated, including their entire bloodline. This is always reasonable if anyone interferes with the shogun's control.

There is little difference in civil or private control; it is always based on desire and the personal ability of the leader. To maintain control in either public or private matters you must understand the rules which you yourself establish for control. You must be quick of mind to change these rules when it befits the needs of the moment. It is also important to understand the temperament of the people you presently command and those you wish to command. Then, with correct action, changes can be made and you can progress to your liking. Under no circumstances can you ever remain passive and static. If you are indecisive you will jeopardize your authority. There are times, however, when your strength can be reinforced through leniency, but you should show no indulgence when dealing with dissenters.

It is also a requirement that you come to terms with and appear to be friendly with all of the people in your domain. Your feelings must be sincere when they are expressed, although your thoughts may be grounded in deception. There can be no room for mediocrity in the shogun's thinking. This will permit insolence and subterfuge to develop which must be guarded against wholeheartedly with regard to both friends and enemies. It will also permit flatterers to interfere with your decisions.

Flatterers must be especially guarded against, but they can be used to your advantage by deceiving their affections. It is better to use them if you feel they have any value at all, and it doesn't matter who they know or the power they may think they wield. If they are useless, rid yourself of them.

Remember, if you will, when Nobunaga Oka was governing Miai Province. He constantly found himself surrounded by well-wishers who only sought to maintain their own positions when Emperor Antoku gave him special consideration during the Taira reign. The people in his domain continually sent him gifts of all types entreating him to intercede on their behalf with the emperor until Oka became enamored of himself. It was then that he found himself unable to deal harshly when it was required. He soon lost control of the government, fell out of favor with the emperor, and was deposed by his own generals. They saw he was not being sincere with anyone, including themselves, unless he was approached with a gift. Nobunaga's acceptance of flattery led him to arrogance, and he thought he could demand anything of anyone in his court. Eventually, no one would heed his orders. In dishonor, he was requested to commit suicide.

If you are in power then everyone must know you are in command or simply, you are not. If you maintain control in this manner, all the people will think they are deriving advantage and enjoying your personal guarantee. If you do not act in such a manner, you may be considered weak-minded, and it will cause your downfall. Everyone, myself included, should be used as a tool for the realization of your greatness.

There are many things to know, and there are many things to learn. It is a never-ending process.

Chapter Two

Private and Public Domains

*I*t is easier to maintain private control than to supervise a public undertaking. If the controller of the private enterprise does nothing except keep the status quo of the hereditary hierarchy, nothing will make the people rebel against him. If change is made in a private domain the members of the clan will seek to assist the leader in an endeavor to maintain their own prosperity based on the leader's new vision.

Maintaining private control takes two factors of acquisition into consideration. One is by ascension through normal inheritance. Changes in leadership are maintained as private affairs throughout the domain that they are directly concerned with. The other is through outside negotiation such as marriages and mergers under any guise. You accomplished one type when you took the Lady Reiki as your consort. Her father was honored by your choice of his daughter and gave you extensive lands as a gift to celebrate the arrangement.

Each of these situations presents benefits and difficulties for maintaining control of the governing factors. When control of a private clan is passed from generation to generation, the common people will consider themselves fortunate in having a benevolent leader still rooted in the original family structure. The nobles of that clan generally will not feel the same way since they are not the absolute leaders. The common people will tend to live in peace accepting their lot in life, and care must be taken that not too much liberality is introduced into their lives. They will not understand such gifts, and if they get them they will not know what to do with them. It is better to keep them slightly suppressed, which should not be confused with oppressed. The people must also know that any outside interference will be taken care of by the leader. It is likewise important to restrict the freedom of the nobles, but that must be done with great consideration to prevent interfamily conflicts.

If misfortune besets the leader of a private domain then the people will rise up and defend their clan, especially against outside threats. Even if the leader suffers from a peculiarity of character, the people will tend to see it as part of the leader's nature and it will be overlooked. Unless he begins to torment the people they will do no more than complain about him. As well, if they feel they are being treated too harshly they may seek outside intervention.

When outside intervention seems necessary, another in the hereditary line of succession can be granted permission, usually by the leader's family itself, to wrest control and change authority. The new authority will more than likely put things back in order and will probably promise new conditions to the people. These promises may not necessarily be delivered or deliverable, but the people know they are incapable of taking control and will acquiesce accordingly. Of course, should there be serious complaint, the development of a faction can occur, causing further trouble where it tends to stir the people to revolt. That person or persons responsible for the unrest must be removed from office. This is not an act of cruelty. It is an act of maintaining control by intelligent means.

This is not so in nonmilitary affairs where people can become quickly annoyed with anything the leader tries to develop. The shogun may inadvertently create a problem that he is unable to rectify without harsh action, whereas in the private domain the leader can revert back to the original idea of the enterprise with little difficulty, unless he commits a severe breach of conduct. In public matters a leader can be constantly assaulted and forced into compromising situations, which may bring an unwanted change in conditions unless he is ironfisted. If he is, the above problem will probably not develop.

To remind you of this situation, please remember when Yoshikai Bento sought to favor his own family with court positions and overlooked the desires of the emperor's family. He gave everyone of his bloodline positions of authority and entirely overlooked the consternation of others more closely aligned to the emperor. The incompetence of Bento's family became legendary, and he was soon replaced himself when the emperor, who had been lenient, was constantly assailed by reports of ineptitude. To alleviate the condition and to put things back in order, the emperor removed Bento and replaced him with the empress's brother. That her brother was also incapable did not matter as much as the tranquillity that was restored to the emperor's household.

The public domain is the entire realm inclusive of private matters. All matters public and private concern the shogunate. The entire country comprises the public domain because it is legislated by the overall rules of the entire society. It doesn't matter who appears to own anything. It is only by the grace of the emperor that the people may have their own lands. Because of this, men will want to please those in control, regardless of the manner in which that control has been appropriated. The people will be happy in mind and spirit when they know they are governed by a benevolent leader.

Because you and the emperor may have differences of opinion, it can become necessary for you to change policy at any given time. You should get an agreement from the emperor and advise your subjects that the change is due to divine intervention. In this manner you won't be looked upon with disfavor by your own people. It will appear that you are only following the directives of the emperor, and you must never show any form of disdain when you are doing this. As a wise shogun, you will understand the powers expressed by the emperor, and you should permit your own actions to please him as well. Regardless, your own ideas will eventually be put into play, permitting yourself to control the entire domain without interference if you are astute. This includes using deception to maintain your position of authority.

Deception is an art naturally developed as one of the most important qualities of leadership. It permits you to remain alert to sudden changes in the domain as to who may be silently creating dissension. Should you determine any distractions that can keep you from attaining your goals, remove them. Awareness of conditions makes it easier to root out those who would usurp the shogunate for any reason.

The general population is easily maneuvered into thinking along the lines of those who are in power. Once the people are assuaged and under control, differences in policy can be easily implemented. There will be no confusion among the masses as to who is in charge. They will agree with the strongest, and they will do so out of fear—your benevolence notwithstanding.

There can be no lack of growth in the future development of the domain. The people must be kept busy or their idleness will degrade into irreverence. If this is allowed to happen they will develop fantasies of power that they do not know how to use. This will permit others with designs upon your position to gather the discontented to their side, creating additional difficulty for you. This cannot be permitted to happen and should be stopped the moment it is detected, without regard for the consequences visited upon those who created the problem.

Current and accurate information is essential in order to maintain control. If information cannot be determined to come from actual fact, then it is suggested that you consider the occurrence of the rumor to be reason enough for quelling any potential disturbance. There is always some truth behind any rumor. If someone shows a desire to wrest control from you they should not be lightly overlooked. Detractors must be removed from office by any means you deem appropriate.

Sugiwara Michizane, a regent in the Fujiwara clan, was unjustly accused of having illicit relations with one of the emperor's consorts, the exquisite Lady Chiba. Michizane was sent into exile even though no one could actually prove that he had disgraced the throne. The cause of his downfall was his overbearing attention towards Lady Chiba whenever she was in his presence. Rivals, jealous of his position at court, spread rumors that created great difficulty for Michizane. His wife committed suicide because of the disgrace that befell her family. The emperor, although unable to prove anything, had no choice but to remove Michizane from the court in order to maintain the dignity required for the proper conduct of state business. No one ever knew if any impropriety was committed.

In a private endeavor a leader can withstand constant attack as long as the resolve to maintain control is evident. He is generally more respected and loved by his clan than the public official—who is constantly under scrutiny because of everyone's belief that they can do a better job if only someone would give them the opportunity.

Public endeavors represent completely different requirements for being governed. People are fickle and do not maintain loyalty if they see any variation in their leader's conduct that can be construed as personally detrimental to them, whether true or not. Very few members of society have any idea about what governing a society entails. If people have specific rules of conduct and regulations for their general freedom, then they will think they are free. They will not feel free, however, if they are actually controlled by external sources that do not give them guidance. The true free society is governed by the laws and rules developed for the specific purpose of the people not having to be concerned about government controls. This condition has never occurred in history and probably never will, but the concept is worth considering.

Public domains must be ruled firmly or chaos will result, orders will go unheeded, and there will be no controls. The entire domain will fall into disrepair even if it maintains an appearance of functionality. If the leader is weak the citizens will be wrought with fear. A new leader taking control during these times will possibly be a tyrant. This usually goes against the nature of the original environment and can lead to a dictatorship, which in itself can either be good or bad depending on the behavior and consciousness of the people.

Public domains are constantly under scrutiny by every member of that society, and there will never seem to be unity or accord anywhere within the realm. For this reason the population of the majority of public domains never cease to be amazed that inefficiency rules the day. The iron fist of a wise shogun is essential.

Chapter Three

Combining Domains Creates Natural Dissension

There are many reasons why two or more groups may join forces. It can be owing to the demise of a clan leader, the conceptions of all groups involved of expanded growth and prosperity, or anything else that man is capable of thinking about to his advantage. When there is change in the structure of leadership there must naturally be dissension among the participants. Someone must take charge, and that authority cannot be challenged. The leader of the domain being taken over must be removed from office once the agreement is accomplished, and he can never be made a partner. That being established, the following must be considered.

People will do whatever they think is necessary for their own safety and convenience, without regard for the rest of the population. Understand this. You will inevitably make enemies of the leaders you have usurped even if the newly established conditions first seemed agreeable to all parties. People dislike change unless they institute it themselves. Actions can include overthrowing their own leaders in hopes of attaining a better life for themselves. When more than one person assumes control of a situation, neither can readily come to terms with it because of the lack of direct leadership.

You can be sure you will injure many of the old regime when you restructure it. You will have undoubtedly made certain promises that you now deem unnecessary to keep. This is exactly what a strong leader must do when he is taking control. You must never relinquish your authority. It will mean nothing to anyone if you do, and can only cause additional confusion. There will always be dissension among the usurped group when they realize you are favoring your own people, as you absolutely must. Likewise, it is foolish for the people being taken over to think you will do otherwise, but that is their problem, and you must not allow their feelings to interfere with the attainment of your goals. Always be on the alert for detractors.

Because there is inherent weakness in any new structure until it is set in place, you must be sure to satisfy the needs of your own people first, even while assuaging those of the new people you have taken on. The authority of your own captains must be reinforced so they do not lose heart when difficulties arise. This is certain to happen in the formation of a new domain, even if it is built on the strengths of older, time-proven tactics. It is essential to understand the ways in which the usurped clan was governed. If a loose hierarchy was in place, see that your own people do not infringe too harshly upon the restructured group. If the old regime was ruled with rigidity, it is easier to maintain that same structure without granting any additional liberties.

Shinchi Kozo, a high-ranking regent of the Miyawa clan, was not aware of the problems he would have to face when he took control of the dissipated Okoni clan. Kozo felt that he could leave things as they were, believing everything would continue on as it had in the past. Members of the Okoni clan were very happy that Kozo thought along those lines, and they continued on with their lives as they had prior to his intervention. The emperor, seeing the manner in which Kozo was operating, decided that certain readjustments should be made concerning the lack of proper controls over the Okoni and ordered Kozo to remove certain of his administrators. Needless to say, Kozo was suddenly faced with problems from both sides of his office. His lack of decisiveness enabled certain Okoni elders to wrest control and to establish an underground movement designed to violate the emperor's edict. It took strenuous effort to realign conditions to the favor of the emperor. Fortunately for Kozo, he was a favored cousin of the court and was given another opportunity to restructure the clan's leadership. However, because of his lack of demonstrable authority, the Okoni were able to keep a significant part of their clan intact, much to the dismay of the emperor.

It is best to do two things when creating or taking over a domain. One is to completely extinguish the ruling order of the old clan. This includes changes in leadership throughout their ranks. The other is to see that no new impositions are put into effect at the outset. If the conquest was hostile, then there is sure to be resentment. If the resentment is handled properly, you will not have to unduly concern yourself with further encumbrances.

Even if the conquest was tranquil, there will still be fear among those newly acquired as to the uncertainty of their future. They will respond accordingly and do whatever they have to do to protect their personal situations, without regard for you. When they are comfortable about the changes in their world, whether they like them or not, then, and only then, should you judiciously bring about the changes required to restructure the environment. People who are unhappy about the situation will generally leave by themselves. They may seek to form new alliances in the hope of eventually overthrowing you, and their potential threat should be dealt with as quickly as possible. Others should be removed for the slightest provocation, and this must be done without warning to them. If you take your time in changing the old regime, alliances can become empathetic. These alliances may be formed between both the new and the old groups. This is to be avoided at all costs, and any breach of loyalty must be swiftly dealt with.

In situations where the philosophies that you introduce are completely different from those of the clan you take over, it is best to be present there yourself. The people will know they are being watched and will seek to protect themselves by fulfilling your demands. Moreover, people from the old regime who have been given authority are not going to willingly jeopardize their own positions in the new enterprise by being overzealous about the old order of things, if they know you are at hand and their future is at stake.

You must maintain a strong disciplinary attitude by visiting all of the locations in your domain. A competent contingent of your own staff should be placed in all areas. Not to do so indicates a lack of control. If the old operation is running smoothly and it is noticeably profitable, then no changes should be made until the new primary directives are in place.

Your captains should understand this, and all changes

considered must first be discussed with you before they are implemented. This is easily accomplished through ongoing meetings with your staff. Failure to do so will permit a potential threat to your authority. It is never wise for you to make change simply for the sake of making change, unless there is an appropriate reason to do so. This is difficult to determine at the outset. Arbitrary changes will cause the troops and officers of both clans to be overly concerned with their personal needs. This can cause operational failure regardless of the shogun's directives.

The shogun must never show weakness in resolve. This will cause a lack of cooperation throughout the entire domain. A strong leader must evoke the respect and fear of those being taken over. They will quickly realize the need to cooperate fully for their own personal reasons and for the success of the overall enterprise.

You must weaken the authority of those temporarily left in charge, without being obvious. When the old guard is weakened, they must be immediately and firmly deposed, so there is no need to fear reprisals. When they are removed, the remaining populace will consider themselves lucky to have been overlooked and will quickly forget their previous loyalty. Therefore, they too will be weakened and will not seek to overthrow the new rule. They will not have the inner fortitude to do so. If you determine that something is left over that can cause trouble at a later time, that situation must likewise be removed. Detractors must be made to see that any attempts at revenge will be foolish and personally costly, even to the degree that they may be unable to earn an adequate living.

Insist that your officers foresee the possibility of eventual discord among the newly taken clan. Provision must be made in advance to quell any potential disturbance. It is true that to prevent a problem from erupting one must prevent the cause. However, once the problem has surfaced it is usually too late to do anything about stopping it, outside of fierce reprisal. This can be costly enough to bring the new enterprise to a halt until the problem is settled. When this happens it is generally necessary to revert back to the beginning in order to reassert your controlling authority.

In Heiji Province, when Morito Takahashi took command, he felt that his presence alone would be enough to quell any disturbances that may have been brewing among the newly conquered people. He did not take the precautions necessary to alleviate any potential threats because he did not understand the culture of the Heiji peasants. They were completely under the influence of their previous leaders and were told by them to act as if they were complying with the new governor. When Takahashi attempted to change conditions, the people naturally revolted, but without showing any disrespect. Being astute, Takahashi realized he would have to learn about their ways and instructed his captains to infiltrate the common people and find out how and what they really thought about things. Doing this gave him the information he needed to eventually place his controls into effect without further inconvenience. When he came across detractors he disposed of them without heeding the complaints of his advisors. In this way he ruled for twenty-six years and was always in the emperor's favor.

Even if it seems prudent not to force a confrontation with those of the old regime, it should be noted that time does not heal all wounds. Do not listen to so-called advisors who suggest that conditions will in time improve for the attainment of your goals. You are the main influence on all conditions, and if you do not take this position, you will constantly be beset by negative circumstances.

Never permit an associate to become an equal in any endeavor, especially when it involves issuing orders to subordinates. This reduces your authority and causes breakdowns in communications. Only one person can be in charge, and if that authority is in dispute, the breakdown will extend to the lower ranks. One person will suggest one thing and another will express a different point of view. This will cause disputes among the leadership, and the workers will react accordingly by using excuses to blame one or the other leader for their failure, and rightly so. They will not know what is expected of them and they will not be free to work effectively. Instead of being productive, they will fear displeasing either of the leaders. They will do shoddy work in the hopes of assuaging both.

Equal alliances are not viable unless the actual responsibilities are defined and in place with no possibility of disagreement. This can only be done at the outset of a venture, when both parties are clear about their individual responsibilities and the mutual goals to be attained. If responsibilities are not clearly spelled out a partnership simply will not work. Someone will always try to maintain authority over the other, which will naturally cause fighting among both leaders, especially when one begins to dominate the other due to the natural development of an individual personality. It is best to accept the fates by making your own decisions, regardless of the outcome, knowing that you are responsible for your own destiny. Errors in maintaining control must not be over-looked or lightly considered. They are to be noted and thought about deeply. I beg your indulgence to permit me to repeat them.

1. If you are going to remove the weaker powers in the newly acquired clan, then they must **all** be removed without favor-itism. They must not be relegated to positions of lesser author-ity, as this will cause them to rebel against your authority.

2. Never permit anyone from the old regime to become stronger by trying to assuage them into becoming your ally. They will see your move as one of weakness and will plot to deceive you regardless of your good intentions.

3. Do not bring in another to act as your equal under any condi-tions once the takeover has started. They will think they have the power to do as you do and will cause disruption through-out the enterprise.

4. You must be sure to maintain offices in newly acquired terri-tories, and your presence must be noted. If you do not do this, your lack of immediate control permits others to act on your behalf. You must be available to your own administrators. The outgoing group must know the foolishness of any reprisal.

5. You must install captains who will report to you with due dili-gence, and you must make sure they are acting in strict accor-dance with your wishes. If they do not do exactly as you direct them, they are to be replaced without further thought.

6. Of utmost importance is to understand that a conflict must never be avoided in the hopes of preventing a breakdown

between your own personnel and those of the newly acquired domain. All this does is permit your enemies to strengthen themselves at your expense. They may then be in a position to take control when you are involved with other projects.

7. A shogun who enables another to come to power in his own domain is himself looking to lose his authority. When an outsider (and everyone who is not **you** is an outsider) is permitted to utilize authority without your express permission, he will eventually assume to have that authority on a permanent basis and will turn it against you. It is the nature of men and the world.

Chapter Four

The Granting of Favors

*F*avors are a perfectly acceptable form of dispensing benevolence when the value of granting them is understood by the shogun and the recipients. The very nature of a favor intimates possible ingratiation by the recipient and must therefore be correctly dispensed. The person receiving the favor must be made to understand its value, as well as the unspoken obligation accompanying it.

It is important to realize that the granting of a favor brings with it inherent animosity, albeit sublime, by the one being granted the favor. This is because the recipient knows that in time the favor may have to be repaid, even though it benefits him at the time of its being granted, and he may be unable to accept the responsibility of returning it. For this reason you must insist that it is your personal desire to grant the favor, while making sure to intimate that nothing has to be thought of concerning its return, while at the same time subtly suggesting that it may possibly be necessary. This is a double-edged sword and must be wielded carefully.

Joshu, a warrior of great repute, was a man of fervent religious belief. His only desire was to be of service to his liege and to follow his own heart in his meditations. He was constantly beset by others wishing him to apply his skills on their behalf, which Joshu mistakenly thought was his natural province to do. He would sometimes have to prevail upon others to assist him in certain matters when he felt they were obligated to him. At first, those he had helped felt pleased to be asked by Joshu to assist him. Eventually they thought he was becoming a nuisance and relegated him to the position of a fool, forcing him to lose face in the eyes of those he had helped. People he had helped began to know of each other's obligation and many embarrassing situations developed. It is wise for you to remember this.

The granting of a favor should be kept completely secret, even from those that are fulfilling an obligation to the shogun in its execution. They don't have to know the reason for the request. If they do, it can give them leverage against you. This can necessitate your having to call upon others to alleviate a condition. When that happens, close friends can suddenly become acquaintances. Therefore, when a favor is granted, it should be done with the attitude that you will never require its return. In such manner you will maintain the power and authority over those graced by your benevolence. You will also have the recipient under your thumb.

Chapter Five

Further Thoughts on the Wielding of Control

A domain is held and controlled by only one person who maintains total dominance. He is aided by handpicked subordinates from his own clan and certain members of the old realm who can use authority only by virtue of his grace. The shogun's authority is ultimate and must be known to be so among his men. When they know this, only the foolish under his leadership would try to usurp him.

Seconds in command usually have no vested interest in lineage. However, it is important to sustain their loyalty by adding to their personal worth. Anything less will not hold weight over a period of time. Specific and exact limits of authority must also be determined so that their self-importance can be more easily controlled. Subordinates must never think they have the authority to make policy decisions. That is your responsibility and yours alone.

Never confuse a desire for personal ascension with friendship. All subordinates must maintain respect for you on a military decisiveness level, as well as that of a personal nature. This has nothing to do with friendship. People maintain loyalty only when they realize it enhances their personal profit, therefore it is not wise to mix the business of ruling with friendship.

Your officers must not be permitted to employ any means without your final edict. They can only become a hindrance once they realize you look upon them with what they will consider special grace. It will also give those thinking they are so favored a license to practice incompetence, and this they will undoubtedly do if you give them assignments beyond their ability and comprehension. You are the only one who can make executive decisions on policy. Not to do so will damage your authority. Exercise great caution in the delegation of authority and responsibility.

One of the reasons that General Noboyuki of the Taira clan was able to keep his court under control was because he was able to discriminate between the personal endearment of his friends and the ultimate prospects of success in his dealings with the Fujiwara. If one of his men who might be a personal friend showed signs of indecisiveness, Noboyuki would immediately replace him, regardless of the fact that there was a close tie between them—even if it severed the friendship. He thereby relieved anyone of the responsibility of issuing orders distasteful to themselves, such as ordering the death of the enemy. His ability to be discerning gave him the reputation of being merciless and a general to be feared. As a result he never lost his authority.

It is wise for you to know your men and the tools with which they perform their duties. Their abilities and comprehension can only become evident if these two qualities are given outlets for expression and can be observed. Being shrewd, you should realize their shortcomings and use them to your advantage. They must also be made to know that failure may cost them their court positions, and possibly their lives, if their true competency is known and they do not live up to expectations. By preferring to maintain loyalty without having to worry about losing their prestige, they will want to increase their skills and will want you to be aware of individual and particular abilities. Generally, they will seek to impress you with their desire to do more than they are capable of doing. This keeps them under control and permits you to elevate them according to your needs based on their performance. Regardless of their rank or past experience, they should never be automatically trusted to complete your instructions without supervision until you are confident that they can make the proper decisions based on your needs. When you have decided that they are ready for advancement, you must still maintain checks to ensure that they are delivering the results you are seeking.

Once the new domain is acquired, the people will have no one to rely on for their sustenance and will readily follow your new regime. They will have no way to reinstate their old ways because they won't know who to put in charge. No one will have had the experience, and among the lower ranks there will be no trust or faith. They might have been fiercely aligned with their previous leader and would have done anything he asked of them, but once he is removed, they will have great difficulty trying to determine the best manner in which to sustain themselves. This enables you to take control without much effort. Once the initial difficulties of the takeover are dealt with, you should have no problem with maintaining control.

Taking control of a domain is accomplished by knowing the rights of succession maintained by the group being taken.

Everyone with any authority at all has his own little province within the overall structure. The members of the group are most likely to be sincere toward you based on their own requirements and your acknowledgment of their self-importance. Loyalty is always based on personal gain. Nothing else!

When taking over a domain you should have little difficulty if you have planned correctly. Nothing should be left to chance. Align yourself with those who find disfavor with their present conditions, which have been imposed on them by the outgoing leader, but remember, there is never a guarantee that anyone will completely submit to your new demands. Blood is thicker than mud.

Although new alliances may appear to be strong at first, especially in the formulation of the takeover, those sensing they will be eliminated will attempt to thwart your efforts. They will try to utilize the talents of those who do not think they will be deposed. Detractors will not have much of a problem accomplishing this, unless they try to align with those who prefer you over the old leader. Regardless, the situation will always result in much political intrigue. It is wise to remember that alliances are based on personal need and not necessarily loyalty to a specific cause. If the newly acquired domain does not entirely accept your leadership, there will be constant turmoil. Make sure to terminate all the members of the previous ruling hierarchy, including those among your own men if they have outlived their usefulness.

Before you established headquarters here in Kamakura, it was necessary for you to meet with the local leaders and determine if any hidden difficulties could arise. The people knew you by your reputation and were clever in their assessment of the conditions that could befall them if you felt so inclined to deal harshly with them. Because you included them in your plans and were understanding toward their needs, you were able to accurately determine the proper manner in which you would take control. Knowing of your astuteness and your warlike nature, they attempted, although feebly, to prepare adequate defenses. By your observation of their movements you were able to thwart their efforts and weed out those of your own staff who were sympathetic to them.

There are three ways to acquire a new realm.

1. Completely destroy it along with any remnants of the people's past experiences and thereby forgo any profit—this accomplishes nothing and is indeed a waste of time, effort, and energy.

2. Leave it to its own devices and only take profit in the form of tribute. This is difficult, and verification of facts is unreliable—men are not quick to give accurate accounts of their actions unless coerced into it.

3. The most intelligent and productive way—live among the people and profit accordingly.

In a domain where the people are accustomed to having personal freedom based on the indulgences of the previous leader, the unwise shogun will leave it under the control of the original ruling group. He does this in the hope of maintaining a cordial relationship, which in the best of cases is impossible. It does not profit him anything to act in such a manner. There is no reason for him to have taken the domain if his thinking was to assuage through neutrality. Thinking in such a manner will set him up for failure, as it is based on the hope that things will work themselves out peacefully. Hope is the lack of true belief and conviction in oneself. People who hope are seeking friends and not great accomplishment.

People seek leadership in any form they can get it and will pay handsomely for it if they think it suits their needs. This will substantially profit the new regime if it is presented correctly. If people realize they are paying tribute but receiving nothing in return, they will feel oppressed and will seek to undermine the new regime. This is a very dangerous situation, and you will find that you are living vicariously through insincere flattery. You will overlook obvious signs of danger to your authority and control.

The only intelligent method of maintaining complete control is to live among the people personally or to set up offices within easy reach. If you remove their old rules as well as their old rulers, you will find them contemptuous if they do not have a presence to observe. Either destroy and rebuild or move in and restructure. Anything else is foolish and a waste of time.

By giving them a reason to continue their existence under your benevolence, the people will rejoice that they haven't been oppressed or put to death. They will respect you as the new leader, regardless of the fact that they are being forced to change their lives. That they are changing their lives for your benefit is not important for them to openly know.

It behooves you to show them generosity, but only if it benefits you. As an example, if they had always wanted the old leader to build a temple for their use and it wasn't done, you should do it immediately if you can fund the project. This puts them off balance and gives them something to be thankful for, instead of resenting the idea that they are now under the control of another leader who could quite possibly present living conditions worse than they have ever experienced.

Understand this, my Liege! Let the people have what they want even if you don't give it to them. Although you may not deliver what you promised, they will live under the guise of hope. People's hope is something that the wise shogun must never permit himself to be manipulated by. Hope is for the weak-minded and not for the builder of empires.

Chapter Six

Controlling and Managing by Your Own Ability

When you attempt to accomplish something great, you must understand all of the aspects of truth in the accomplishment of these gains. Regardless of your ability and because you did not create the universe, imitation (to a degree) of the actions of great men who preceded you is essential. If it should happen that you do not have the intrinsic qualities of those who went before, you can still establish goals that will approach great accomplishments. If you do not ascend to the levels of your desires because of difficulties, natural or otherwise, ambitious dreams can still be realized. This is best done when a man uses his own talents and resources and does not rely on others. A man's personal desires become obvious to his enemies when they realize that he will have nothing to pay back to anyone. Outsiders will see the foolishness of interfering with him.

Shunko Zabayashi knew the importance of using his own resources when he effected a coup against his cousin in Tarama Province. He carefully thought about his actions before moving into position to take control of the clan. Although his cousin was a man of wealth, he was a squanderer, always insulting others who had less than he had, he would throw lavish parties and cause dissension in his own court by inviting certain people and excluding others. Zabayashi observed that many members of the clan were beginning to resent his cousin. Slowly, he built up his resources of men and funds until he knew that his cousin would be hard pressed to stop any advance. Forgoing the pledged assistance of others, he moved when he knew the time was right, and because he did not rely on the aid of people who would follow him regardless, he maintained control of the clan for the rest of his life and was never indebted or obliged to anyone.

Accomplishment is based on definition and redefinition of goals, which has to do with good fortune and good planning. Good fortune usually accompanies determination and desire. Good planning is always better. As much as is humanly possible, nothing should ever be left to chance. Careful examination of the works of great men will show that they did not rely on the inconstancy of fate. They saw opportunity and took it because they were emotionally and physically prepared for success. As a result of this mentality they accomplished great things and prospered. It may be necessary to strive hard, but once the goal is attained it is very rare that it will be lost. The man of merit understands that he will be surrounded by those of little faith, even among his most ardent supporters. This lack of faith will continue until the new order is established, at which time it is prudent to dispose of the nonbelievers.

It is also necessary to realize the need for material strength in the acquisition of a new domain. Without the proper armaments and supports, failure is guaranteed because of the inherent or residual strength of those being taken over and the natural resistance of change. You cannot win with spirit alone and the hope of success in the future. You must be prepared to do serious battle, and you must have the resources necessary to accomplish your ends. These resources must be your own, or you will have to pay back in kind those that support you. They will be waiting and watching for your first indication of weakness.

Sometimes it is required that uncomfortable alliances be permitted to exist in order for the man of vision to attain to his accomplishments. When this time comes upon the builder of great things, he must know no limitation to his patience and the acceptance of aid, until he is in the position of eliminating those who would turn into detractors.

People must be shown without hesitation or restriction the advantage of accepting your authority. You must force unbelievers to believe in you by demonstrations of inner strength and managerial ability. With this there can be no hesitation on your part. You must act with total conviction and absolute authority. Anything else will permit a usurper to destroy you from within. Those who would seek, through words or actions, to undermine the new regime must be taken from their place of self-importance, regardless of how small their insolence may at first appear. If left unchecked they can grow into great encumbrances.

In an authoritarian society any demonstrated weakness will be aggressively sought out by pretenders to your office. This is another reason why you cannot rule from afar. You must have nothing else on your mind except your success, and you must make sure to stand apart from your under-lings—their good wishes notwithstanding.

It should be realized that when a new order of things is introduced, enemies of all types will emerge from places known and unknown. Even those who are sympathetic toward your rule will be only halfhearted, until they see the new order enhancing their lives. It is sometimes easy to persuade others to your way of thinking because of the newness and novelty of the potential new order, but it is only with force and authority that their belief is sustained. It is foolish to think otherwise. Everyone is in accord with his own thoughts, and the ideas of the new leader may not wholly coincide with the people's personal desires. There are no friends in combat, and any form of personal development that will leave others behind is indeed an aspect of combat and a requirement of greatness. Even a lover may defect for reasons that are beyond ordinary comprehension. Beware of those you align with for any reason.

Chapter Seven

Assistance from Without

ll people cannot be leaders or commanders nor should they be. Most people who desire authority are unstable in their own cause, and therefore it is not natural for them to lead. Most people have little desire to attain to greatness and have little stomach for the harsh reality of acquiring those ends. They will tend to be lazy regardless of their professed love for you. Even if they follow you resolutely, they must be observed in the performance of their duties. There is no telling when fortune will coerce them toward rude thinking with regards to your welfare.

When taking over a domain, think in terms of building from the ground up by establishing proper roots and supports for your goals. The roots of a great accomplishment must be examined and studied constantly to seek out any flaws that could undermine further development. A lesser attitude seeks its own destruction because of the project's inability to maintain itself. Limitation of thought must be guarded against at all times. You must be of great resolve.

Men of great power and determination, regardless of who they are, enter into periods when, for unexplainable reasons, a manifestation of weakness may evolve. This is not to be feared as it may be a fortuitous omen in disguise, indicating your ascension into a higher realization, which will further your accomplishments. Turn these times of self-introspection to your advantage by recognizing and using them intelligently. Remember, no man is invincible, and there will be times when your mind will seek to impart new wisdom through what might appear as confusion. When you see yourself becoming weak you must immediately take action to correct your thoughts.

Men of skill have their own sense of worth and may sincerely not desire to be the shogun. They must be recognized and held closely to the leader's breast, regardless of whether or not you necessarily like their attitudes and dispositions. These men must be permitted to approach you with due respect and personal intention. Intuition is of great worth in these matters.

Tomiyo Kubataro, the chief architect of the Emperor Goshu's court, was noted for his brilliance in constructing pavilions and mansions for the royal family in Kuzo Province. He never thought of being better than anyone, only wanting to do the best he could. One day he was visited by the empress and was given a commission to build a new temple to house a sculpture of the Buddha. He thought about it but could not come up with an appropriate design and soon fell into a tremendous gloom. None of his old designs would work properly, and he was at a loss to understand why. The day before he was to have an audience with the empress he decided to wile away time sketching and meditating on Buddha. Suddenly he realized that he had drawn a completely new design, and when he showed it to the empress she was taken aback. Knowing of his reputation she permitted him to build it. It was completely different from anything that had been built before and has now stood for over six hundred years.

Power and authority based on proper planning will permit you to employ quickness in your decisions. Strength and speed are not to be confused with power and quickness. Strength and speed are based on a man's physical ability. Power and quickness are based on his mind's acceptance of himself. If they appear to be the same to you, then perhaps you do not fully understand your ultimate goal, regardless of the lofty ideals that presuppose it.

Because of the nature of the universe and the need to be assisted in endeavors of greatness, there will be times when you will require the assistance of outsiders. Not to do so indicates limited thinking in understanding how to truly attain your goals. No man can stand alone regardless of his strength. When accepting the grants and favors of others, be of the mind to accept the probability that you will have to pay back in kind everything you have borrowed—usually with interest. You will have to grant favors that could interfere with the attainment of your goals.

People who bestowed favors on you will demand more and more as time goes by, depending upon the success of your endeavor. They will also have the attitude that they are the actual driving force behind your ascension and will at times prevail upon you to acknowledge their contribution. This is as it should be. You should not think in terms of denying those who helped you. Jealousy can appear from the most unlikely of places. You must eliminate this possibility and control the condition rather than show signs of weakness by acquiescing through ingratitude.

Deception is the most important quality of a true leader. Irrespective of the consensus of popular opinion, once the usefulness of a particular party has been determined to no longer be of value, scandals and embarrassments must be brought to bear against them. This will immediately limit their power and create a divergence that must be dealt with in an attempt to maintain their court positions. They will be humiliated if they cannot quell these disturbances and will be embarrassed to face you. Deception also creates false opportunities for others who would wish to usurp you in favor of their own gains. By employing acts of deception in your court, the sincerity or falseness of those attached to you will become evident. Reward those who remain faithful!

Being of great spirit and appropriate zealousness, the wise shogun can act in no other way. You would not have ascended to your position of importance if you ever thought otherwise. There is nothing inappropriate about destroying the opposition and putting those who remain loyal deeper into your servitude. Those who would remain loyal will generally do whatever they must to protect themselves, and they may tend to agree with everything you say and do. They too must be watched because their personal ambition may be more important to them than yours is. They do this because they realize they could be in line to be replaced. If they are permitted to become stronger they might form alliances from within your domain. Please remember, most people who love you do so out of fear of their own losses. Never trust emotions in the determination of your goals, and do not consider the need to keep those in your favor who seek to go in their own direction. Remove them!

There will be close advisors in your court who will tend to disagree with everything you are attempting to do. It will take a prudent mind to understand their real concerns. If they have proven themselves to be faithful and carry out your orders even though they express displeasure, they are to be considered as staunch allies. As well, their disagreements can be beneficial to you if you see from their points of view. You will be able to strengthen your position because of your ability to solidify your desires based on sincere opposition and not frivolous disagreement.

It does not matter what you do to attain your goals. People who attain to greatness must, by the very nature of their quest, behave in what would appear as less than genuine sincerity. You must have the full faith and conviction of your own belief if you would maintain the position of influence that you desire. The greatest builders in history have had tremendous respect for themselves and have not been concerned with the thoughts and feelings of others. This was especially so when it came to personal self-love and true self-knowing. They were not fickle in their own thinking. They were determined and therefore used whatever means they could to gain, maintain, and sustain their goals. If you do not think in this manner then you are only playing at accomplishment. Do not worry about making enemies; you will certainly do that. Tomorrow you will make new friends and alliances. Sincerity toward others is not a trait of the great shogun.

Detractors do harm through hatred, ignorance, and fear. The wise leader can determine when fear is becoming hatred or if it is truly based on a person's ignorance of the facts of life. You must have the mentality to rid yourself of those who are not sympathetic to your goals or else you will not be able to maintain your focus. It will be easy for detractors to usurp you if you do not maintain this attitude.

Chapter Eight

The Application
of Cruelty and Evil

W hen a man aspires to greatness he must inevitably use cruelty to attain his ends. This cruelty must be wisely applied. Not to use cruelty indicates a lack of purpose. The proper use of cruelty can be used to turn defeat into victory. The intelligent application of cruelty explains things to others without the need for debate.

Cruelty takes many forms and does not always have to be physical. To indicate your attitude of expected behavior from your subjects, the possibility of severe punishment must be in their consciousness. Mental cruelty, if not properly dispensed, can provide an enemy with an avenue of retaliation. The development of previously unknown character traits can help him to depose you.

Torture should never be dispensed with an attitude of arrogance. Physical torture can destroy a man and should be used when applicable. It should be used immediately if no worth is seen in the recipient. And, as with all things, timing is essential. It might be fortuitous for you to be patient and wait until the right time. This requires contemplation.

The application of cruelty and evil also requires an understanding of men, which is something that Noritomo Kenji did not know. Because he was known throughout his realm as a man of severe intemperance, his subjects were always under a threat of physical torture—evidenced by Kenji's handling of any disobedience. He would not think twice when it came to dealing out what he considered to be just retribution and would unconscionably order court suicides and executions that included anyone associated with the person he was angry with. His people greatly feared him and would do anything they could to assuage his anger. They began to lie, give unverifiable accounts of the province, and generally not care for anything related to him. He was eventually decapitated by one of his inner guard.

Your understanding of, and ability to apply cruelty, shows your determination to ascend to the highest levels of greatness, with or without the recognition or assistance of your subjects. This includes your immediate entourage and inner guard. They too must realize the virtue of intelligent cruelty and thereby will prefer to concur with your wishes. If they decide to abandon you they must know you will use whatever means necessary to exact retribution, while at the same time you will maintain the gratitude of those not being injured, regardless of their relationship to the offenders.

You must be sure to be constant in your convictions, and you must be capable of acting on those convictions without hesitation. There are no friends when one attains to the summit; there are only those who will assist if they are guided accordingly. When you seek friends with minds like your own, you are seeking acceptance by those empathetic toward your aspired greatness. This will cause you to weaken yourself.

Dispensing cruelty must be considered a form of virtue; otherwise the act will lead to arrogance, conceit, and false pride; the deadliest of errors in self-definition and self-determination. This is to be construed as truly evil and must be guarded against, lest your subjects act on your orders through exaggerated fear. Cruelty should only be applied when it will gain you an advantage. You must be careful not to permit the application of torture to become a personal pleasure. If it is used callously it will become a device without meaning except to generate terror among your people. You will lose their enthusiasm toward your ambitions.

Torture can be applied in ways other than to the physical flesh. It can be the removal of properties and the restriction of armaments. There are also methods of creating poverty. Once a subject has been deprived of the things necessary for him to conduct his affairs, he will have a hard time persuading others to lend him support to regain his position. The application of torture must permit the shogun to sustain his authority. Cruelty must be used to indicate that your actions are just and that those who would assist the deposed will suffer the consequences.

Once you make the decision to apply restrictions to a subject, he must never have the opportunity of enjoying a reversal of your decision. This will accomplish nothing and will show the rest of the domain that your leniency can possibly turn to indulgence. This will cause the people to seek to overthrow your authority. You must rule with an iron fist. Compassion should only be used when it is appropriate, perhaps based on the possibility of misunderstanding that can only be excused once. You must be wise and have deep intuition.

There is a great difference between cruelty and evil. They should not be confused with each other. Savage and barbarous acts do not enable a man to be counted among the truly excellent and wise. While it may be necessary to depose the nonsympathetic by any means, you must differentiate between gaining control through terror and being respected by your subjects. This is accomplished through elements of fear or cruelty and not through acts of barbarism that will perhaps temporarily enable you to maintain control. If you are unwise in dispensing justice to your people, an avenue will eventually present itself for your overthrow by underlings, which can result in a reversal of your own fortune.

Kishi Noritaka, the chief constable of Harama Village, is a perfect example of not respecting his own domain and causing his own downfall. It was the most foolish of situations that brought him down. The Lady Hana, his consort, was indiscriminate in one of her alliances, and news of her unfaithfulness reached the ears of Noritaka. He reacted in a most hideous way by having the lady publicly punished in front of her clan. When he had finished humiliating her he demanded that her body be left on display in the poorer section of one of his villages. I do not have to elaborate on the manner in which her body was disrespected. Noritaka continued to publicly disgrace everyone in her clan until finally the lady's cousin, Nobuye, took revenge on Noritaka and had an assassin decapitate him. It would have been much smarter for Noritaka to have had her hair cut off and then banished her to a monastery where the punishment could have been less physical but certainly more severe and lasting.

Deception is not considered evil unless the means by which it is employed destroys the foundations of the newly acquired clan and its environs. This is not self-serving to your cause. Although deception is necessary to instill obedience, you must be sure to maintain the good faith of your subjects. Random and senseless acts of killing those not in agreement with you should be restricted to those indicating overt gestures of rebellion. Actions must never be gratuitous. Such behavior indicates a weakness of character in the shogun. The need for evil increases instead of lessens as it must, unless the correct application of controls are established early at the outset of the acquisition.

One way to bring corrective measures to the new domain is to recognize and acknowledge the injustices perpetrated by the old regime. That these injustices must be alleviated is essential, and it must be shown to the people that they were evil. This reinforces your position by maintaining ease of control at the outset, when the people see you are sincere in alleviating their hardships. Your actions on their behalf must be carried out as quickly as they are determined to be detrimental. This reduces the fear that occurs if correcting conditions take place over a long period of time. If it is done correctly it will throw the people into a state of chaos, and they will see the advantage of following you. If you are not swift in your decisions it will be necessary to maintain a defensive position at all times. If your actions do not fall into sensible patterns of conduct, your ministers will wonder when your wrath will fall on them, and they will act accordingly. It will also permit those being acted against to forewarn others to take up arms to protect themselves in the eventuality of your vengeance or instability.

It is better to have change over and done with quickly and suffer the anxiety of the moment, rather than needlessly tormenting the people over a long period of time. When punishment is meted out over a long period of time, those that feel they may be in line for corrective action will become clever in their attempt to cover themselves. When punishment is meted out too late the results are never virtuous. Do it all at once and get it over and done with. The resentment of the people will be short-lived as they will have no further concerns for themselves. They will believe the new shogun took care of all the potential problems. They will feel they are fortunate not to have been part of the scourge.

Regardless of your good intentions, and even if cruelty is dispensed intelligently, it will still be considered evil by anyone associated with the receiving end. It will be acknowledged as an unnecessary evil and not the necessary cruelty that your wisdom will dictate.

Chapter Nine

The Emperor's Good Graces

Once you have proven yourself to be of an absolute necessity to the people, you must continue to act in accordance with the entire country's needs. There must never be any variation from this ideal. In this manner you will remain the shogun and will have the respect and honor of the emperor as well. The position of shogun is attained with guile and intelligence in order to seek the greater good for all—including yourself.

You must take care not to be overly clever as this will result in having to watch your back at all times, which will interfere with intelligent governing. Note that nobles do not wish to be governed by any means, especially through oppression, and the common people do not wish to be oppressed by the nobles. Everyone must be made to feel secure, and everyone must be made to feel important for the overall good of the emperor—not the shogun.

It is always better to be loved by the common people and to be feared by the nobles. The nobles will always be jealous of your position and authority. It is wise to show that any acts leveled at the people, nobles and commoners alike, are brought to bear by the emperor's edict.

There will always be more common people than nobles. They will listen to you wholeheartedly if you show them consideration and exhibit no overt favoritism toward the nobles. The common people will always be the common people, and they cannot be replaced. However, the nobles will know they can easily be replaced should they fall into the emperor's disfavor. It doesn't take much insight to realize that the army is mostly made up of common people.

The proper way to view nobles is with judiciousness and caution. They will either be with you or against you. Those against you will seek to denigrate you in the eyes of the emperor. Very few will be neutral. If they are with you it is because they seek advantage for themselves and generally will not have the heart for rebellion, unless they are goaded into it. They should be used wisely to further your own good fortune. Those who are against you should be considered with great care: you must be sure to know when they are of a mind to try to depose you. Those whom you feel would try to depose you, for any reason, must themselves be weakened and deposed by any means necessary. This must be done before the emperor is required to intercede.

The emperor will always be watching and always has the authority to replace you. Whether or not he has the resources to do that is not the issue. There is always someone in the emperor's court who is trying to bring about change for his or her own benefit and who will bring in outside influences as allies. Emperors are human beings even though we acknowledge them as gods. They have frailties and weaknesses that must be recognized by the alert shogun. It is wise for you to be readily visible to the emperor, at the same time ensuring that no possibility of a faction is rising against you with or without the sanction or mandate of the emperor. If the emperor is pleased with you then he is also aware of your worth, and he will seek to have you act further on behalf of the entire domain. A shogun must be a master politician. Lie to everyone but back yourself up with the emperor's good graces.

Men will always side with their benefactor when he rules with justness. Nobles can create internal dissension and farmers can poison food. Without either one you tread a dangerous path. It is best to assuage the nobles by maintaining control over them through promises (whether delivered or not) and to the common people who only wish to be unoppressed. Seek the goodwill of all in your domain starting with yourself.

If you can maintain harmony between all of the people you will be seen as a man of rare wisdom. You will be obeyed and respected by all in your domain. If you favor a particular group they will eventually seek to overthrow you because of your overly relying on them. Nobles must always see you as ruling on their behalf to increase their fortunes. The common people must always see you ruling in their favor by making their lives easier. If people, irrespective of their rank in life, think they are happy, they are.

Chapter Ten

Resources

*I*t is important for the shogun to have his resources intact and not to have to rely on others in the event of an emergency. Adequate money, manpower, and arms are necessary to field an army. The shogun must be able to take to the field himself and not have to hide behind his fortifications because of any lack of supply. If the shogun is seen as self-sufficient, other men will be hesitant to take to the field against him. They will recognize him as adequately capable of defending his domain.

Toriyaku, a general of the Fujiwara clan, did not have the necessary resources to prevent the Taira clan from overrunning his domain. The Fujiwara clan leaders were always remiss in providing the supplies to stave off an attack. It eventually became the crux of their own downfall. When supplies were of the utmost importance they couldn't be delivered. The Taira had completely surrounded the village and nothing could get through. When the Fujiwara armies finally did appear, the Taira had already overrun the village. The Taira were well fortified and used the village for their own fortification until their additional forces came and completely annihilated the Fujiwara.

Authority must be maintained with great zeal. Zeal is always required for the safety of the domain. It is wise to use zeal when building your resources and supplies even in times of peace. It is especially during times of peace that would-be usurpers will determine their chances of success in challenging your authority. When building up resources, be in harmony with your suppliers. Rule with tenacity in order to show your strength and resolve. You should supply your men with weapons of the newest design. And you should ensure the unavailability of them to anyone else. New devices should be tested against a neighboring clan as suggested to you by the emperor if possible. The shogun will be guided with intelligence when he hears the emperor's choice. If the emperor prefers not to be involved, the shogun must make the choice.

New weapons must first be tested in training and then in actual combat. At the same time, make sure that backups of old and time-tested methods are at hand to quell any unexpected problems. You must attack with force and authority, showing everyone your capacity to completely destroy an enemy. If there is indecision on your part, the enemy will try to draw out the action in an attempt to drain your supplies. This must not be allowed to happen. It is increasingly difficult to field an army and keep them idle for extended periods of time. The objective is to get in and get out quickly with total domination of the situation, thereby pleasing the emperor. It is therefore wise as well to keep your troops constantly training and to have them ready to deal with any situation at all times.

Men will always feel bound to give service equal to the rewards they receive. Also, if they see you are not resolute in protecting them, they will seek security with the opposing forces. If for any reason you are unable to rise to the occasion or deign to defend the country, the people having made sacrifices on your behalf will expect compensation in any form they can get. If none is forthcoming they will join with the new forces to throw you out.

Chapter Eleven

Religious Beliefs and the Soul of the People

hough not generally thought of with much introspection, the religious beliefs of a newly acquired
domain should be given consideration when
determining the manner in which that domain will be ruled.
Religious beliefs are rooted in ancient laws that far surpass
the desire for personal gain of either nobles, more than likely,
or the common people, certainly. It is not wise to slaughter
the priests and raze the temples unless you are of the mind to
totally destroy the culture. You should depose all that is necessary, but make sure not to destroy the temples or religious
retreats if you would ever profit from the conquest.

Do not destroy religious artworks, or for that matter secular artworks, unless they are deemed inflammatory. All art
represents the soul of the people. To destroy a man's home is
one thing, but to destroy the nature of his Ideal is to cause
him to rebel with great anger. Though force can overcome
the insurrection, the disadvantageous result will be that of
turning the population into nonproductive slaves who will
then have to be constantly prodded to do their work. It is
better to completely annihilate an entire population if that is
the case.

In the year 963, Michizaki Hotei descended upon the
province of Surugawa. Being a man of little faith in religious

matters, he immediately destroyed all evidence of the people's ancestors and their beliefs in the hereafter. The people of the province were terrified by Hotei's actions and revolted by not complying with any of the general's wishes. They constantly foiled any attempts by Hotei to bring them under subservience, which they may not have done if he respected their ideologies and incorporated them into his plan for control of the province. Eventually, Hotei had to leave the area because of the embarrassment he was receiving from the emperor in regards to not being able to control the populace.

You should seek to enhance the religious beliefs of the people and with such action show them that the takeover is in their best interests. In this manner the people will see the benevolence of the new leader and will rush to aide and assist him once their own leaders have been deposed. Men can easily be replaced, but only with great difficulty can gods be replaced.

Artists, both religious and secular, reflect the emotional consciousness of the people. Musicians, painters, sculptors, and poets are the soul of the people. If they must be deposed the action should be carried out quietly. If the action is carried out publicly there is good chance they will become martyrs. Do not destroy their works unless it is absolutely necessary. By keeping the works available to the people, a certain spirit will be maintained that will not permit the people to become forlorn and depraved.

Chapter Twelve

Mercenary Troops

*T*he shogun must maintain troops to protect and preserve his domain. It is essential to understand the necessity of sound government, the application and installation of stable laws, and the fairness of the regulations. Troops are used for the protection of the domain and the enforcement of the laws. These troops can either be your own men or they can be hired mercenaries. They may be used singularly or mixed to achieve the desired end result. It is always best to use your own troops without having to rely on mercenaries because of the inherent lack of faith and discipline of strangers. Mercenaries tend to become arrogant and can be very discourteous to all, including the shogun, when they are idle. When mercenaries are mixed with loyalist troops there will usually be discord among both groups. The loyalist troops may not understand where the shogun's heart lies. It is not wise to mix loyalist troops with mercenaries.

Mercenaries are generally unreliable and will wait to see the most advantageous time for their deployment. They may have to be provoked into action, possibly by severe means. This means an internal conflict to be dealt with along with the external. Little will be accomplished and the cost will be great. At best, mercenaries can never have more than a passing interest in the quality of life promised to the domain and its citizens. Mercenaries will show no true devotion to your aspirations and will care only for the money they receive, which is always inadequate in their estimation. They will never think they are being properly rewarded. If you have no alternative but to use mercenaries, you will be under the constant strain of guarding against them.

If the mercenaries are skillful they will always seek to gain advantage for themselves and will without fail attempt to intimidate you. If they are not skillful they will still cause problems because they may be unable to carry out, either by inability or by design, your orders. The shogun must absolutely lead his troops in combat or the hired men will seek to do things as they see fit, including making alliances with the enemy if it suits their purses and purposes.

It has been proven time after time that the only way gains can be maintained with authority is if you use your own troops—rewarding and punishing accordingly. If gains are made they will be solidified by the loyalty of your own men following you into battle. Their fighting spirit will be fierce because they will fight with resolve to protect the interests of the domain. With mercenaries it is the reverse. The gains will be slow and labored, and the defeats will be resolute and crushing. At the first sign of problems the mercenaries will seek to save themselves by any means available, including jumping to the other side.

When Kicho Matahara was enlisting troops to overwhelm the fortress at Negimahara in the days of Emperor

Kammu, he felt it would be in the best interests of all concerned if he had an extra contingent of men from Yamashiro
Province to reinforce his troops. When he approached the
leaders of the Bakufu clan to enlist their aid, they readily
agreed to join with Matahara but only if they could share in
the spoils of the battle. Seeking to please the emperor,
Matahara agreed to the terms and made plans for the attack.
The Bakufu general approached the Negimahara fortress and
laid bare the plans of Matahara in order to make a better
arrangement for his own people. The Negimahara clan
accepted the Bakufu as allies, and when the attack began, the
Bakufu troops switched sides in the midst of the battle,
bringing serious defeat to Kicho Matahara along with great
dishonor. The emperor was fortunate to have wiser generals,
and they were eventually able to save the day, but not before
Matahara committed suicide.

If it becomes necessary for you to use mercenaries, specific rules and restrictions must be in place to prevent muti-
nous activity. The problem here is that you must use your
own troops to enforce the laws. If you have troops to enforce
the laws then you should be sure to have enough troops
when approaching a new domain without having to rely on
outsiders. Train your troops well and train your troops thor-
oughly. In this way you will keep your new acquisition. If
you do not have the necessary resources and you are firm in
your determination for the venture to succeed, then wait
until you do. This is a matter of knowing who you are,
where you are, and what you are trying to accomplish.
Sometimes it is necessary to sacrifice an immediate gain for

a long-standing advantage. To do this takes insight, wisdom, and clear intuition. You must personally develop these skills, the development of which must be meditated upon with due diligence.

Chapter Thirteen

Auxiliary Troops

A uxiliary troops are generally turncoats from the domain under consideration of acquisition. It is sometimes required that you call upon auxiliaries to achieve an alliance or to accomplish certain goals. They should be considered the same as mercenaries. When approaching a domain, it is important to restrain yourself from using the turncoat troops of the land you are invading. If auxiliary troops cannot be trusted by their own leaders, they certainly cannot be trusted to perform adequately under your guidance. If you use these troops and lose in your attempt to acquire the new domain, the results will be disastrous. You can fall under the sword of the leader of the very troops you borrowed. If you are successful you will be indebted to them, and this will cause additional conflicts. Also, borrowed troops may refuse to comply with the directives being put into place, and, having seen your strengths and weaknesses, they may attempt to claim victory for themselves.

You must regard auxiliary troops in this manner. They can become more dangerous than mercenaries. Mercenaries may be cowardly and deceitful in their intentions, but the auxiliary troops will have been trained more directly in your ways and are therefore capable of causing additional conflict.

It is always better to lose with your own troops and understand the reality of the loss than it is to win with the assistance of foreigners. The wise shogun will build his own forces adequately.

If you will remember the Battle of the Plain of Shisei, you will bear in mind that General Hijiro Shujo gave much thought to his plans for attack, though he was greatly undermanned. This did not sway his determination. Knowing the domain was ripe for the taking, he reinforced his own troops with those of the other side that would see their own leaders fall. He could have diplomatically taken the land through negotiation, but he preferred to strengthen his military position by rattling his swords with turncoat troops. His conquest was immediate and without trouble until he attempted to impose his authority on the newly acquired land. Because he was outnumbered by the auxiliary troops, they immediately turned Shujo's conquest into a defeat by turning against him to further their own gains, which was the reason they joined with him in the first place.

The astute shogun should not celebrate the victories of the auxiliary troops. Instead, he should create difficulties for them as he approaches his goal. This alleviates the possibility of having to fight the very people he used to gain his ends. It is also plausible to turn his own troops upon the auxiliary forces once the goal has been attained and in that manner gain conclusive control. This is an ingenious strategy, and only the most intelligent shogun, such as yourself, should attempt to apply the tactics required for its success.

Never praise auxiliary troops in front of your own men.

They may become disheartened and think you are faulty in your love. Denigrate the auxiliary troops after they have served their purposes, and do it with clever ploys. If you have used troops from an alliance that has proven itself to be stronger than you are, then you are in effect using mercenaries with an attitude of hiring neighbors. It doesn't work.

You must show force and authority at the right time and with proper resolution. You must also turn the auxiliary captains away from the original promise of returning their lands to them. Do this in the prescribed ways of depriving them of their authority and strength. Using the arms and equipment of others puts you in their obligation, and should you fail to be victorious, you will be hard-pressed to maintain your advantage.

Chapter Fourteen

The Shogun's Concern with Military Matters

*A*ny attempt to gain anything brings with it the need for conflict. This must be completely understood because without proper planning a predisposed acceptance of defeat is cultivated. The only reason a man becomes a leader is because of his desire to see his dreams accomplished. This self-knowing attitude is always met with resistance from sources known and unknown.

The shogun must understand conflict and must have enough self-discipline to be successful in his mastery of it. The rewards of success in conflict bring with it the attitudes of fine living. If the shogun thinks little of additional gains after his initial successes, he will invariably experience defeat in one form or another. Instituting action requires the heart and mind to see it through to ultimate accomplishment. Any other thinking is a waste of time and resources.

If you become ignorant of the need for further military activity once you are in control, you are beckoning to the fates to take away your gains. Once the action is put out of play, others will seek to take it away from you. It is the natural order of things. If you become enamored of the easy life, you will find your winning spirit will never be a match for someone with many swords. Your men will also see this weakened condition and they will lose heart. They will not follow you with conviction when you issue orders, although they may do so out of fear. Men need authority in their lives regardless of appearances to the contrary. They must be told what to do and when to do it, even if they think they are their own persons.

The shogun must know the qualities of all the common men, including farmers and artisans as well as merchants. All embroider the soul of the land into the hearts of the people. Farmers must be cared for so there is an ample supply of food for troops when they are in combat or are training for it. Artisans are the craftsmen of fine weapons and will always have an attitude of insolence. They should be put up with but never given positions of authority. If they become an annoyance they are to be treated as any other subversive. Merchants keep the economy of the land flowing. Deal with them most carefully as they tend to be the most disingenuous.

There are two ways for the shogun to maintain the domain in times of peace and in times of conflict, and both are of equal importance. One is the physical exercise of going out into the field to examine the conditions of his men. By joining with them in lesser social activities he can determine his troops' resoluteness. Can they be depended on or are they getting soft? Are they enthusiastic about protecting the domain and expanding it? The shogun can see the mentality of his men by observing them firsthand. The other is to study the accomplishments of great men who have come before him and learn how their empires were built. They will have left records of their accomplishments which will be easy to attain. Even by listening to the songs of the people much can be learned.

The first method permits the shogun to visit with his men in places that can maintain him in peak mental and physical condition. This also permits him to see flaws in his fortifications. He sees who is weak and who is strong. He sees who is maintaining the proper ideal of the domain and who is simply playing at it through superficial works. He will soon come to know those who are doing their jobs and those who are devoted to their work. There is a great difference between the two. Those who maintain the ideal are to be rewarded, and those who do not are to be retrained or deposed.

People who do their jobs well are usually not concerned with appearances. True work is not labor; it is joy. It is how one receives pleasure from within, knowing that the job is being done to perfection according to one's abilities. Those who labor without sincerity always complain about their tasks and of never having enough supplies. The wise shogun knows that if men labor insincerely, they are not working for the benefit of all.

The shogun maintains his domain through continually studying the accomplishments of men who came before him. Common men and most nobles will not perceive what the shogun perceives. The shogun studies the entrapments and the successes of those who came before him. He studies the methods his predecessors employed to accomplish their ends. He studies the ways great men built their great works and he adopts many of their attitudes into his own mind. He becomes that much more effective as a ruler.

Minamoto Yoshiie, your great-grandfather who founded the Kamakura government, knew of these things. He would constantly visit his troops in the field to see how they were holding up and at times even celebrated with them, of course, within the constraints of his office. He always carried a book with him and continually studied the ideas of strategy by the Chinese scholar and warlord Sun Tzu. He never permitted himself to make an abrupt decision without first thinking carefully about the condition of his troops, and he never gave himself the idea that he was above any further learning. This is why he was revered by all of his men and had their complete support when he founded the government.

The great shogun will accomplish great deeds because they are his work and not because he is doing his job to impress others. If he seeks to impress others he will certainly fall.

Chapter Fifteen

Why Shoguns Are Praised Little and Blamed Much

*F*ortune and men's minds are not generally aligned with each other. A man who constantly seeks to do good will by the very nature of his acts come to ruin. This is because most people are not good unless it is to their own advantage. Goodness is usually temporary at best. If a man is good all of the time, others will see it as weakness and play upon it to their advantage. The wise shogun knows when to switch attitudes without regard for his personal feelings or those of others who may seek to curry favor based on their own perceptions.

Nothing you do will ever be construed as praisable by everyone. Those who think in terms of evil will find a way to undermine your good intentions. The manner in which men live is completely different from the manner in which they should live. When men cannot approach harmony of thought they will always find someone other than themselves to blame for their shortcomings in life. If they were wise men they could be leaders, but not having that desire, they will present no conflict aside from the petty annoyances they can muster among themselves. With common men, who else is there to blame but the shogun? With nobles, who else is there to blame but the shogun? You must never permit yourself to be overwhelmed by the desires of the people, especially if those desires do not coincide with yours. As well you must never permit yourself to be overwhelmed by your own desires.

You should rule with an iron fist and destroy anyone who would seek to usurp you. In this instance, or any like it, you will be considered evil. You should not care one way or the other as to how people think about you. You are the leader and they are the subjects. If they cannot accept this, they should be asked to leave the domain, and if they are hesitant to do so, they should be assisted. As shogun, you should be concerned with others' thoughts about what is good or evil in the minds of the people, but you should not permit their judgments to interfere with your decisions. Simply act on your best behalf, putting fear into anyone who would disagree with you to whatever extent you feel is prudent.

Minamoto Yoritomo, you are our leader. It does not matter if the people love you or despise you. Their feelings change like the wind depending upon what you deem necessary for maintenance of the realm. Your own mind is the mind that carries the day forward—for all concerned. You have yourself seen that all men are subject to their own wiles as did Yoshifusa when he married Emperor Saga's daughter. Everyone knew the reasons for his marriage including the emperor. That did not stop Yoshifusa from eventually controlling the empire while being completely unconcerned with the thoughts and feelings of the rest of the clans.

Regardless of what you do, you will never please all factions at all times. This is why the growth of domains is ever slow to progress. If one man thinks the shogun is wise, another will think he is stupid. If one man thinks the shogun is being open about a matter, another will think he is being deceptive. There is no limitation to the fault men can bestow upon their leaders. You must always hold to your own counsel or you will not remain shogun for very long.

Chapter Sixteen

Generosity and Miserliness

M any people in the court will always have different opinions of you regardless of your deeds and actions. In the same manner that you must be lenient without becoming noted for indulgence, you must rule your people with a tight fist. If you are not tightfisted, people will think your generosity is something they have coming to them. They will presume this for no other reason than by association with you and their asking for it. If prudence is maintained, you will be seen as miserly, which is a much better thing than spending your resources through generous deeds. You will have to levy taxes, and the people will come to despise you, even though you are giving them the things they want.

Because generosity is not a truly virtuous thing, and its practice cannot be observed without becoming dangerous, it is always best to say no when approached for special consideration. This is not the same as being asked for favors. If you feel the request has merit, you can always change your mind later and fulfill the request.

In time, because of your miserliness, you will come to be seen as a man of wisdom, because you will always have the needed resources for maintaining the domain without seeking outside assistance. Because your resources are not being squandered, your fortune will flourish. The common people will love you when they aren't required to pay increased taxes. And the nobles will be pleased that they aren't being asked for additional funds to subsidize the government.

Miserliness is a virtue of intelligent governing. The shogun should never spend his own money or the money of his people. When establishing control over new domains, make sure to extract tribute in any of its many forms. In this manner you control the domain's resources. Remember, things grow within their own universe: liberality breeds intemperance as miserliness breeds wealth. Liberality will spend itself out until there is nothing to be liberal with. Miserliness will maintain itself by not permitting expenditures for anything that is not considered truly necessary.

In order to rise in power and greatness it is important to spread gifts in the right directions and for the right reasons. People think in terms of what they are being given and shown. They will give you support because your generosity will help them preserve and increase their own power. However, once your goal has been attained, miserliness must be the rule of the day, and your generosity must be shut off. This accomplishes two things. First, it sends a clear message to those who assisted you in your rise to power that more is expected of them if they wish to further partake of your benevolence. It doesn't matter if they think they are being manipulated, because everything you are doing will be shown to be to their advantage. Secondly, now that they know more is expected of them, they will be more inclined to act in accordance with the new rules or suffer the consequences.

Yoshikawa Todai, the wealthy merchant of Haruma Province, is one of your most loyal retainers, and as you remember, when you were preparing to march against the Sumitomo clan he immediately came forth and offered to give you, not lend you, any amount you would need for the success of the military operation. He did this for any number of reasons including that you had seen fit to make him your chief supplier of armaments. In your wisdom you felt it would not be wise to become indebted to a merchant, and instead you told him to take whatever money he would lend you and place it in the proper hands affording him the ability to get whatever he needed to supply you. Todai's contacts felt they were in your favor, and after giving Todai what he requested they tried to make deals with the Sumitomo clan based on their thinking they could even the sides and disrespect your station. Todai's bribes came to an abrupt halt when he saw what they intended to do, and because these other suppliers were without funds to develop their businesses, they shortly failed and came under your complete control.

Power is the best part of being the shogun. It must be handled intelligently.

Chapter Seventeen

Looting and Raping

When a shogun is at the head of an army he must show his men, by his actions, that he has their well-being in his heart. If they have followed him into battle and have conducted themselves with dignity and honor they are to be amply rewarded. But never at the shogun's expense.

By permitting your men to share in the prizes of a recently acquired territory, you show your men that the riches to be gained are to be shared among all of them. Knowing this, your men will follow you even further, becoming hardened to the aspects of danger in coming campaigns. Take your share of the booty, of course, but make sure the rest of it is spread among the troops. Be sure to replenish what you spent on the campaign and to increase your personal worth, but the rest should be meaningless because you are assured that more will come as new domains are acquired.

The warlord Genghis Khan always instructed his captains to completely massacre the total population of any new territories he was invading. He insisted that everything of value should be taken and shared among his men. He also advised that the raping of women in a newly acquired territory was essential in the long run holding of that territory because the results of a conquest are evident when the offspring of the enemy are in the likeness of its conquerors. The overwhelming strength of the conqueror will be shown in the bloodlines and will make the possibility of future revolt that much more difficult. He intuitively knew that the people would accept the new culture thrust upon them and rejoice that they had become part of a stronger society.

Do not listen to the weak-minded who advise you that looting and raping is evil. If your advisors are trustworthy and yet remain adamant, you should ignore them while noting their dissension. Their hearts may be in the right place but their minds certainly are not. The disharmony they bring about can affect the holdings of the shogunate. If they become overly vocal in their objections, quiet them!

Chapter Eighteen

Revenge

evenge is a virtuous act, and its intelligent application is an essential quality to a powerful shogun. However, revenge does not work without difficulties, and although it appears to be profitable at certain times, it is best carried out long after an incident has been quelled. Even better, revenge can be applied most effectively when the event has been practically forgotten. When it is dealt out to those requiring it, it must be done in a fashion that deeply impresses everyone—from the emperor to the common serf. It must be done in such a manner that any ideas of duplicating the act would be thought of as madness.

In time, the strongest warriors will be subject to foolish behavior regardless of the amount of care taken to prevent its occurrence. Attacks come in many forms and are sometimes difficult to discern, especially when you are in the position of delegating authority to subordinates. Revenge is usually necessitated by acts against the shogunate from the inner guard. The problems may stem from without, but usually the damage is instigated from within, and more than likely by trusted subjects.

Care must be taken that you do not become obsessed with revenge. You must not become mean-spirited. There are two ways for revenge to be exacted. One is quietly, dictating terrible misfortune that no one could have foreseen. The other is done openly, and with a terrible effect, guaranteeing that no one would ever consider a like act against you for the remainder of their lives. The method depends upon your temperance. It must make itself evident to all who are aware of the reason for it.

The person at whom the revenge is directed must remain alive to see the horror that is visited upon him. He must be the last of his bloodline to be destroyed regardless of the method used. The punishment meted out must be so complete that no possibility of reprisal is possible. Things that can be done to others as acts of revenge are only limited by the imagination. Revenge should be extracted with such a degree of horror that the perpetrator's ancestors scream from the grave.

Ishikai Nobunaga was a master at levying revenge. For deeds done against him by his wife's family, he began a reign of terror against them that lasted for years until they were finally wiped from existence. The reason they carried out their acts to wreak his revenge were founded in terrible jealousy of his position in the court of Emperor Kicho. But their acts were nothing in comparison to the penalty they paid for their insolence. He began slowly, and long after the deed against him had been perpetrated, by causing them to dispute rumors from within their own houses. When they came to be filled with anger at each other, he then began to destroy their means of livelihood, making each of his wife's cousins appear to the other as a thief, eventually forcing them to devise acts of retribution against each other, culminating in bloodshed. They even came to him hoping he would assist in quelling the family problems. In essence, they gave him permission to further break down their bloodlines. When they were totally weakened he watched as they finally destroyed each other.

It is always best to permit your enemy to kill himself. Halfhearted attempts at revenge invite retribution and must be avoided at all costs. It must be done in a matter-of-fact manner. Physical revenge should be delayed until all other means have been executed. To crush the spirit and destroy the offender's mind is the best way to begin. Death should be saved for last. In the beginning, techniques of revenge should include minor inconveniences and petty annoyances building up to a thorough deterioration of the antagonist's body, mind, and spirit.

Chapter Nineteen

The Absolute Necessity of Protocol

Two types of protocol must be observed or a break-down in the chain of command will ensue throughout the domain. The military structure is one in which it is generally accepted that commanders pass order and directives from the top down. There is not too much difficulty in understanding the need for protocol in this arena of activity.

The second, and even more important protocol, is court protocol, without which everything completely falls apart, including the control of the army as well as the entire government. The shogun must demand absolute deference toward himself and his inner guard without ever permitting deviation. This is difficult to maintain if there is no set code of conduct adhered to by everyone, regardless of his or her relationship to the shogun. This includes his immediate family: his wife, parents, children, his confidants and mistresses.

Nepotism is the biggest problem, followed by any other form of favoritism shown to anyone in the court. It does nothing to enhance the value of the domain unless the heir has been proven capable in the arenas of conflict. As a man of power you will always be approached by those who consider themselves your equal, except for title, as priority representatives to the throne. No one is equal to the shogun, but because you must be approachable, special care must be given to requests from those close to you through bloodlines. These people are usually approached beforehand by flatterers who are very capable in manipulation of powers associated with control.

General Jitto, once he had assumed power in Gayaku Province, decided he would put those of his family into positions of authority, thinking he could keep closer control over the domain. He thought his relatives would be sure to give him honest reports about conditions throughout the province, knowing they wouldn't want to fall into his disfavor. He was sadly mistaken. He found that everyone he had placed, thinking it would be to his advantage because they all would cooperate with each other, became contemptuous of each other instead. His wife insisted that he place her brothers into positions of authority. So did his uncles and his mistresses. Eventually he was kept busy trying to keep the peace in his inner court, while constantly being assailed by the emperor as to why matters were always getting bogged down. Jitto, being a man of intelligence and worth, finally took control of the situation by throwing his relatives out, replacing them with people who had no blood ties to him. Jitto carefully examined the work of each person he put into office, and within a short time he was able to gain back control to the pleasure of the emperor.

While you may have to be benevolent toward your bloodline to keep the sanity in your own household, you must always remember the possibility of personal anxiety. This will certainly affect the sound judgment needed to efficiently govern the domain. It is wise to deal with these potential impediments before they happen by keeping to a minimum the favors you grant to your bloodline. Be certain to keep control of the domain and the control of your house separate.

The reality of court control is the same as controlling any other circumstance and must be seen from that perspective. Not to do so invites intrigue and foul play.

Chapter Twenty

Making Yourself Understood

One of the most disconcerting problems you will ever encounter is the inability of subordinates to understand what you are saying compared to what you mean. This directly affects their performance. This problem must be handled through the disciplined consciousness of the shogun and the shogun alone.

People generally hear only what they want to hear and will ignore that which is not in line with ideas for their direct benefit. You must not permit subordinates to interpret your directives. Spell them out exactly and avoid any possibility of confusion. To do this, it is necessary to study the language and the manner in which your ideas are presented, including correct writing form and articulation of speech.

Many great leaders of the past studied the books of past masters. They had no confusion in their own minds about the need to study continuously. They constantly refined their knowledge and further developed their ideas using whatever tools were available to them for the realization of their true self. When no previous reference was available they invented one.

When you issue an edict or mandate, you should write it down and refine it until it spells out exactly what your intentions are. This clarifies your directives so they are understood by any who would be responsible for what you delegate. By doing this, you ensure proper execution of the edict. Never assume that a subordinate understands what is in your mind. If the subordinate did know what was in your mind, then perhaps the subordinate would be the shogun.

General Hatana was very strong in the field. He could lead his men with simple gestures and never experienced failure in combat. However, when he was invited to the court, he was dealing with people of a different caliber who did not think a soldier was capable of directing circumstances in the court. He would try to communicate with them by intimation and mere suggestion to which they never adequately responded, making it appear that his orders were not being carried out. General Hatana was no fool. He enlisted the aid of the priest Rensho to assist him in learning the ways of the court. Rensho had a very intelligent student, and after spending little time General Hatana spoke the language of the court and directed his subjects with authority and clarity, never encountering the problem again.

Words have the ability to mislead unless their meanings are understood by all involved in the execution of a plan. Instructions must be written and explained in the simplest of terms so there is no possibility of misunderstanding their meaning. They must be spoken back to you to ensure that no misunderstanding exists. Not to do this is to invite failure. Only after many satisfactory experiences with particular individuals can you expect them to understand the spirit of the directive being issued. And then it must still be checked for accuracy. Apply this thinking to all of your mandates and sanctions.

Chapter Twenty-One

Countermanding an Order

 any great men have been destroyed because they could not countermand an order. There are various reasons for not being able to do this, but most important is the fact that perhaps the great man lost sight of his complete goal.

Leaders of merit have no problem revoking a command if the need arises. They are able to do this even though they know they might find themselves in disfavor with their ministers. This does not dissuade them. They know that if their inner guard does not come to understand his change of mind it is all well and good. At times even the inner guard must be kept off balance. If discontent arises and continues, replace the potential detractors. This will keep your other subordinates in line with awe and fear.

When orders have to be countermanded there is a very good possibility that you did not plan properly. When you issue orders to sustain your power, you might overlook a factor that is so obvious that your ministers and subordinates would be surprised. Of course, the fact that they may not have noticed it should not surprise you either. Planning is a multiple-level project, and you must know when to take counsel and when not to take counsel with your inner guard.

All conditions must be studied carefully to prevent conflict in understanding your orders.

Reichikan, a *monchujo* in the court of Emperor Saga, was always hoping to please everyone, and because of this weakness he could not revoke an order, even when it was pointed out to him that it was detrimental to keep it in action. He simply did not wish to offend those who could profit from his edict, including his friends. That he had become *monchujo* through political alliance soon came to be the reason for his downfall. When a certain tax was levied against villagers in his province, for what he, Reichikan, thought was for his own good, the finance ministers at court told him to rescind the order because the villagers were being pressed enough. Reichikan did not heed their advice because he felt his authority would please the emperor. Instead, the villagers revolted, causing Reichikan to lose his merit within the court, and he was soon replaced.

A significant problem that arises when an order is countermanded is that it can create insecurity in the mind of the individual who was initially supposed to carry it out. If you did not give proper authority to the individual who was to carry out the order and you were not ironfisted in the selection of your men, then fear can easily replace confidence. They must be strong enough to understand, not necessarily the burden of leadership, but certainly the responsibilities you have toward the proper management of the domain. It is therefore essential to pick your men wisely lest they become discouraged and think they are in disfavor when an order is changed. Command is not for the squeamish.

Chapter Twenty-Two

The Deadliness of Arrogance, Conceit, and False Pride

When a man has accomplished his goals it is easy for him to slip into the morass of three deadly attitudes—arrogance, conceit, and false pride. It is very hard for most men to avoid this, and it takes a great amount of discipline to control the personality problems that develop with great success. It is at this juncture that you, as the great shogun, will show your mettle and not permit self-flattery to develop.

To be impressed with one's own self-importance is to invite flatterers to think you are permitting yourself to become more important than the work you have accomplished. This is the first step toward personal downfall.

It is especially crucial to the shogun in his maintenance and sustenance of power that he become even more ruthless and more demanding of himself and of his people. This is how empires are built, and the ironfisted mind of the shogun must prevail, driving his people to ever greater accomplishment.

Future planned works must be based solidly on past accomplishments. Nothing can be built from heaven downward. Rather, things must be built from the ground up, and the higher the aspiration the more intense your desire and authority must be. "Shogun" does not mean master. Master, however, includes the station of shogun.

Superficiality is rampant in our society, because men think they have done something special when all they have done is to stand on the shoulders of those that came before them. So they will tend to think that they are responsible for the propagation of the world.

The wise shogun knows better. There is no need for me to illustrate the words in this scroll. They are self-evident. A man of greatness stands on the shoulders of previous great ones permitting himself to see further than they did. He always acknowledges them, perhaps privately, but he acknowledges them. He knows that Heaven has graced him to build great things and to make great works. He acknowledges the Source of All both privately and publicly. He performs the proper rituals for the people to see him giving thanks. In private he falls to his knees in thankfulness that Heaven has seen fit to trust him with matters of wonder and awe. When Heaven sees his true worth, Heaven Itself will prevail upon him to accomplish more.

This way, and only this way, is to live in greatness. It is not a thing for small-minded men.

Chapter Twenty-Three

No-Thing-Ness

What I have attempted to explain to you, my Liege, is certain to be known to you. Not wishing to be presumptuous, I have given you what I believe is the most intelligent and realistic information. I am indebted to Heaven and the grace bestowed on me by God to have been considered wise enough to explain my understanding of these things to you.

What I have discussed is without doubt what a man of your attainment certainly knows. But the wisdom does not stop there. These words are for the benefit of all men in all times, and if they would understand what the words themselves impart, they would truly control their own destinies to the degree that they can accept these truths.

A man's position in life is always based on the degree to which he accepts the values shown to him by the spirit of the thing itself. This spirit reveals to a man only that which he desires it to reveal to him, personally. Spirit is impersonal and could care less about you until you tell it what to do on your behalf. It has no mind of its own and, again, can only reveal of itself as you desire it to reveal of itself. You may of course prevail upon it to show you the way to higher understanding.

To know you are shogun is one thing—this takes learning. To realize you are shogun is some-thing—this takes meditation. But to be shogun is no-thing, and this demands acceptance of the self.

Most people fail in life because they are not aware of the internal power they have or the manner in which they can increase their usage of it. The inner self is impersonal; it is not a "thing." The true meaning of personal development is in the true acceptance of your own personal being. It has nothing to do with technique, which may be good to know but readily interferes with desire because of its reliance on external forms to develop internal realities.

Every time you move your hands or feet, your mind or your tongue, it should be considered an attack and a non-attack simultaneously. Attack and defense are one and the same thing and can only perform according to your acceptance of their functionality. This is strictly dependent upon your devotion to it by way of personal belief and training. If you do not have this understanding then you can only be a puppet, lacking the inner resolve to attain higher levels of consciousness.

Specific technique only enables you to perform adequately that which is necessary to maintain and protect your personal environment. It has nothing to do with your innate skill as a leader, which is completely different. There is always someone smarter, faster, stronger, more devious, and more benevolent. The shogun is what he is: a shogun and nothing else. You must understand what a shogun actually is, and you can only do this by introspection and personal definition. The existence of certain heavenly attitudes and qualities must be accepted on a personal level to maintain you on a specific level of consciousness. This is called "correct thinking."

The shogun does not get involved with ranks or titles, names of styles, who is best at something, or anything that would suggest comparisons with others, including competitive thinking. The personality does indeed play an important part, because without a personality there could be no self-identification. We do not live in a mindless environment, although most people function on that level, and so we cannot exist without references.

To do so would indicate a lack of self-esteem that would deny survival and accomplishment. The healthy personality does not have to brag about its accomplishments—its work is self-evident, and its only purpose is to drive its self to higher levels of consciousness within the structure of any given discipline.

Do not think in terms of experiencing accomplishment, but rather accomplish experience through actions, deeds, and thoughts. This is the true meaning of what is commonly called Zen, which has recently come into fashion. Zen is that which absolutely seeks to negate itself through total acceptance of itself. In the same manner, a doctor practices medicine to alleviate disease; once that is done there is no need for him to be. It is called no-thing-ness.

No-thing-ness is not to be confused with the term nothingness, which is an objective reality, physical or spiritual, supposedly existing in the void as a "thing." Called "Mu," it does not exist and yet must be real so it can be identifiable. A man must get past the need for understanding something that goes beyond the intellect and simply accept oneness with it, thereby becoming the very thing itself.

Again, my Liege, to know you are shogun is one thing,

to realize you are shogun is some-thing, but to be shogun is no-thing, and this demands a true self-knowing of your being. To know, to realize, to be—all is MU.

With true devotion, humility, and respect, I present this to you.

Hidetomo Nakadai
Autumn 1195